METEORS
AND COMETS

EARLY BIRD
ASTRONOMY

BY GREGORY L. VOGT

LERNER PUBLICATIONS COMPANY • MINNEAPOLIS

The photographs in this book are used with permission of: © Boryana Katsarova/AFP/Getty Images, p. 4; © Don Spiro/Stone/Getty Images, p. 5; © Flirt/SuperStock, p. 6; © altrendo travel/Altrendo/Getty Images, p. 7; © Hulton Archive/Getty Images, p. 8; The International Astronomical Union/Martin Kornmesser, p. 9; © Chad Baker/Photodisc/Getty Images, p. 10; © Pete Turner/Stone/Getty Images, pp. 11, 16; © Michael Dunning/Photographer's Choice/ Getty Images, p. 12; © Don Davis/AFP/Getty Images, p. 13; © Richard Bizley/Photo Researchers, Inc., p. 14; © Tony Hallas/Science Faction/CORBIS, p. 15; © Laura Westlund/ Independent Picture Service, pp. 17, 20, 22, 24, 25; © NASA/Time & Life Pictures/Getty Images, p. 18; © Derke/O'Hara/Stone/Getty Images, p. 19; © Mark Garlick/Photo Researchers, Inc., p. 21; © Dan Schechter/Photo Researchers, Inc., p. 23; SOHO (ESA & NASA), p. 26; NASA/JPL-Caltech, p. 27; NASA/European Southern Observatory, p. 28; © Kauko Helavuo/The Image Bank/Getty Images, p. 29; © Digital Vision/Getty Images, p. 30; © StockTrek/Photodisc/ Getty Images, p. 31; NASA/JPL/Malin Space Science Systems, p. 32; © iStockphoto.com/ Stephan Hoerold, p. 33; © Detlev van Ravenswaay/Photo Researchers, Inc., p. 34; AP Photo/ Geoff Howe, CP, p. 35; © Yuri Kochetkov/CORBIS, p. 36; © Odd Andersen/AFP/Getty Images, p. 37; © Philippe Psaila/Photo Researchers, Inc., p. 38; © European Space Agency/Photo Researchers, Inc., p. 39; © Science Source/Photo Researchers, Inc., pp. 40, 41; © NASA/Photo Researchers, Inc., p. 42; © ESA/AFP/Getty Images, p. 43; © Yoshinori Watabe/amana images/ Getty Images, p. 48.

Front cover: © Eckhard Slawik/Photo Researchers, Inc.
Back cover: NASA, ESA, and the Hubble Heritage Team (STScI/AURA).

Lerner Publications Company
A division of Lerner Publishing Group, Inc.
241 First Avenue North
Minneapolis, MN 55401 U.S.A.

Website address: www.lernerbooks.com

Library of Congress Cataloging-in-Publication Data

Vogt, Gregory.
   Meteors and comets / by Gregory L. Vogt.
     p.   cm. — (Early bird astronomy)
   Includes index.
   ISBN 978–0–7613–3876–5 (lib. bdg. : alk. paper)
   1. Meteors—Juvenile literature. 2. Comets—Juvenile literature. I. Title.
QB741.5.V635 2010
523.5'1—dc22   2009020562

Manufactured in the United States of America
1 – BP – 12/15/09

CONTENTS

BE A WORD DETECTIVE

Can you find these words as you read about meteors and comets? Be a detective and try to figure out what they mean. You can turn to the glossary on page 46 for help.

asteroids

atmosphere

coma

comets

comet tail

crater

gravity

meteorites

meteoroids

meteors

meteor shower

nucleus

orbit

solar system

spacecraft

telescope

CHAPTER 1

SPACE ROCKS AND ICE BALLS

Think of the night sky long ago. There were no city lights. Everything was very dark. Thousands of stars shone in the sky. People were comforted to see the stars night after night.

But sometimes, a new star would appear suddenly. It might be a bright flash blazing across the sky. Once in a while, the streak would fall all the way to Earth. At other times, a new star would appear and get brighter night after night. Then it would become fuzzy looking and grow long, hairlike streaks of light. Several months would go by. Then the new, hairy star would fade back into the dark.

A falling star streaks through the sky over Joshua Tree National Park in California.

ISTIMIRANT STELLA   hAROLD

The Bayeux Tapestry is a decorated cloth that was made in the 1070s.
One of the tapestry's pictures shows amazed people pointing out the 1066
appearance of Halley's comet (TOP CENTER). They report it to their king (RIGHT).

These hairy stars scared the people who
lived long ago. People thought these stars
meant something bad was going to happen, like
an earthquake or the death of a king.

People later learned more about these new stars. They are not really stars at all. They are space rocks and ice balls. The space rocks are meteors (MEE-tee-urz). The ice balls are comets (KAH-mits). Meteors and comets are two types of interesting objects in the solar system. The solar system includes the Sun and eight planets.

This picture shows the Sun (LEFT), the eight planets of our solar system, and the dwarf planet Pluto. In reality, the planets are much farther away from one another.

A meteor shines in the evening sky. What are meteors?

CHAPTER 2
ROCKS FROM THE SKY

You can see a meteor on any clear night. A few flash across the sky each hour. Sometimes there can be many more. Some people call them "falling stars" or "shooting stars." But a meteor is really a space rock.

Meteors are called meteoroids (MEE-tee-uh-royds) when they travel through space. Most meteoroids are the size of a piece of sand. Some can be as big as a house.

In Earth's skies, meteors travel fast. They move at about 26 miles (42 kilometers) per second.

This computer image shows a meteor lighting up as it nears Earth. It creates a glowing streak that shoots across the sky.

Meteoroids that fall into Earth's atmosphere (AT-muhs-feer) are called meteors. The atmosphere is the layer of gases that surrounds Earth. Meteors rub against the gases in Earth's atmosphere. They become very hot and begin to glow. That's when people can see them.

Meteoroids are formed in two ways. Many come from asteroids (A-stur-oydz). Asteroids are large chunks of space rock and metal. They are so large that they are called minor planets. Asteroids have crashed into one another for billions of years. These crashes cause pieces of the asteroids to break off. These pieces float through space. Later, they might fall to Earth or to other planets and moons.

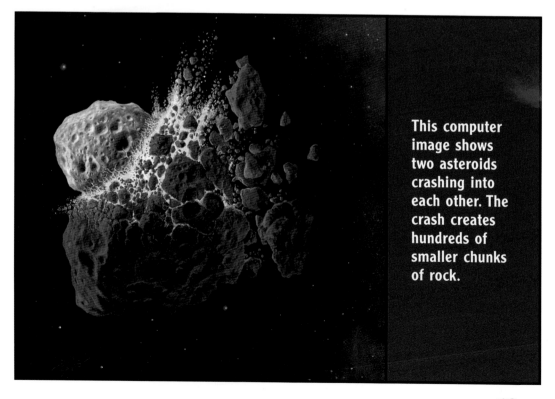

This computer image shows two asteroids crashing into each other. The crash creates hundreds of smaller chunks of rock.

Other meteoroids come from comets. These icy objects travel in a long path around the Sun. Earth sometimes crosses the path of a comet. The dust and rocks trailing behind a comet may fall to Earth.

In this painting, a comet trails a streak of gas, dust, and rocks along its path past Earth.

The Leonid meteor shower appears every November. That's when the comet Tempel-Tuttle passes Earth.

You can see dozens or hundreds of meteors each hour when Earth crosses a comet's path. This is called a meteor shower. Some meteor showers happen at the same time each year. They happen when Earth crosses the comet's path again.

A meteor streaks through the night sky. Bigger meteors are easier to see. They create longer and brighter streaks of light in the sky.

Meteors shoot through the sky about 40 to 75 miles (65 to 120 km) above our heads. Most flashes last only a second or two. Those streaks come from meteors smaller than the size of a pea. Meteors the size of a pea make longer and brighter streaks. Even bigger pieces may get so hot they explode. Really big meteors can be the size of baseballs or even cars.

Some meteors can make it through the sky without burning up. These space rocks that fall all the way to Earth are called meteorites (MEE-tee-uh-ryets). They are made of rock or metal or both metal and rock.

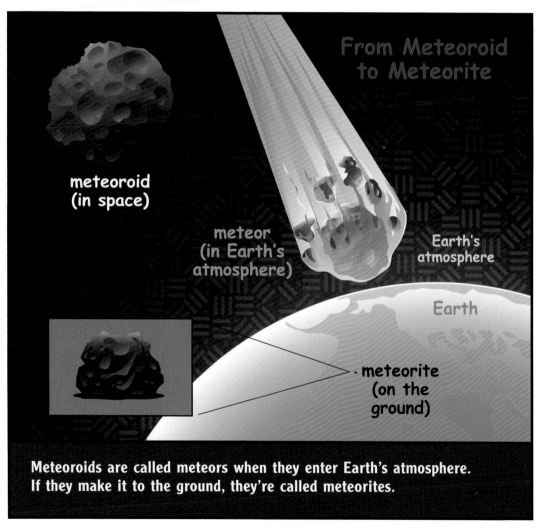

From Meteoroid to Meteorite

meteoroid (in space)

meteor (in Earth's atmosphere)

Earth's atmosphere

Earth

meteorite (on the ground)

Meteoroids are called meteors when they enter Earth's atmosphere. If they make it to the ground, they're called meteorites.

Some meteorites are rocks from the Moon and Mars. Imagine that an asteroid or a comet hits the Moon or Mars. This crash causes rock from the Moon or Mars to fly into space. Some of this rock may drift for thousands of years. Then it finally falls to Earth as meteorites.

Scientists believe that this meteorite was once part of Mars. They think that it fell to Earth and landed in Antarctica about 13,000 years ago.

Comet Hale-Bopp shines over a lake in Arizona in 1997. What makes a comet's tail glow?

CHAPTER 3
ICE CHUNKS IN SPACE

Comets do not always glow or have a tail. Comets are often dusty chunks of ice, sand, and rock. They are like this when they are far out in space, away from the Sun's heat. But comets change as they come near the Sun. The Sun's heat changes them. They warm up and seem to glow. They often form a long and bright

Comets travel in an egg-shaped path around the Sun. This path is called an orbit. Sometimes a comet's orbit is far from the Sun. But sometimes the same comet's orbit brings it near the Sun.

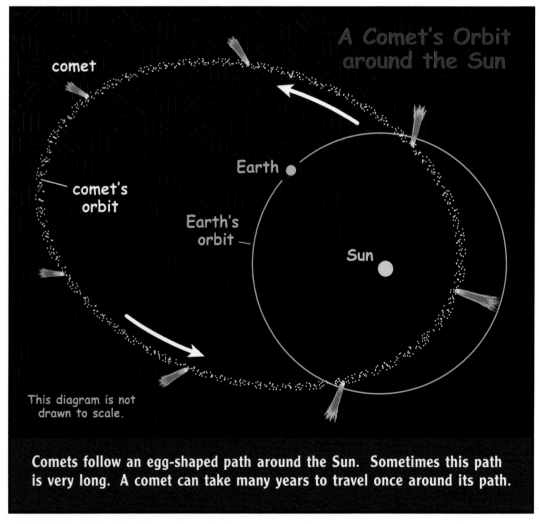

A Comet's Orbit around the Sun

comet

comet's orbit

Earth

Earth's orbit

Sun

This diagram is not drawn to scale.

Comets follow an egg-shaped path around the Sun. Sometimes this path is very long. A comet can take many years to travel once around its path.

The Sun's heat melts some of the comet's icy surface as the comet passes near the Sun. The icy center of a comet is called the nucleus (NOO-klee-us). It can be a few yards or tens of miles wide.

An artist created this image of a comet's icy nucleus. The nucleus may be made of frozen water or other chemicals.

Gas, dust, and rocky grains are freed as the ice melts. They form a cloud that surrounds the comet. This cloud is called a coma (KOH-muh). Some of the gas streams away and forms the comet's tail. A comet's tail can be millions of miles long. Some comets have two tails. One tail is made of gas. It always points away from the Sun.

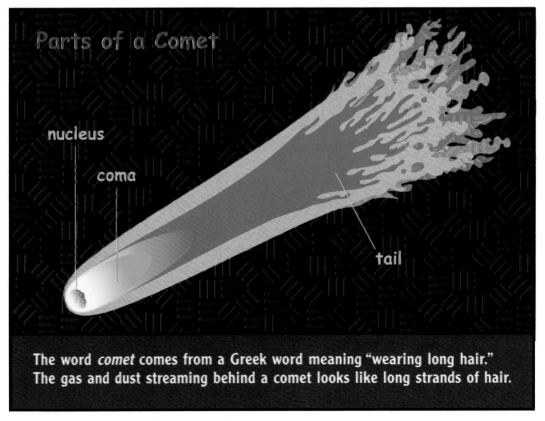

Parts of a Comet

nucleus

coma

tail

The word *comet* comes from a Greek word meaning "wearing long hair." The gas and dust streaming behind a comet looks like long strands of hair.

Comet Hale-Bopp has two tails. The white tail is made of dust particles blown off the comet. The blue tail is made of gas. It will be more than two thousand years before Hale-Bopp passes Earth again.

Some comets' orbits are much bigger than others. Comets may return near the Sun every few years. Or comets may return every few thousand years. Some pass the Sun once and never come back.

Scientists think that probably more than one trillion (1,000,000,000,000) comets orbit the Sun. Most travel from a cloudlike area called the Oort (ORT) cloud. This area is about 100,000 times farther from the Sun than Earth is. Other comets orbit much closer. They come from a place near Pluto's orbit. This place is called the Kuiper belt (KY-pur behlt).

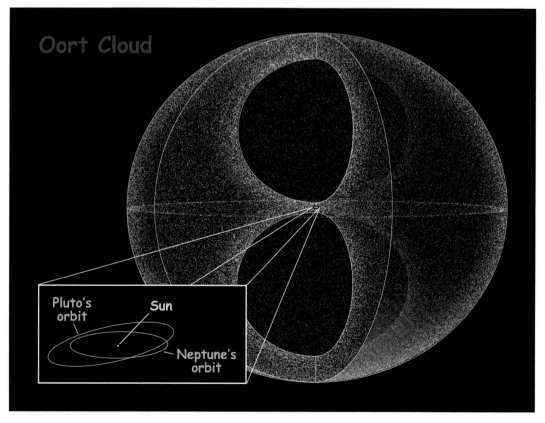

Oort Cloud

Pluto's orbit

Sun

Neptune's orbit

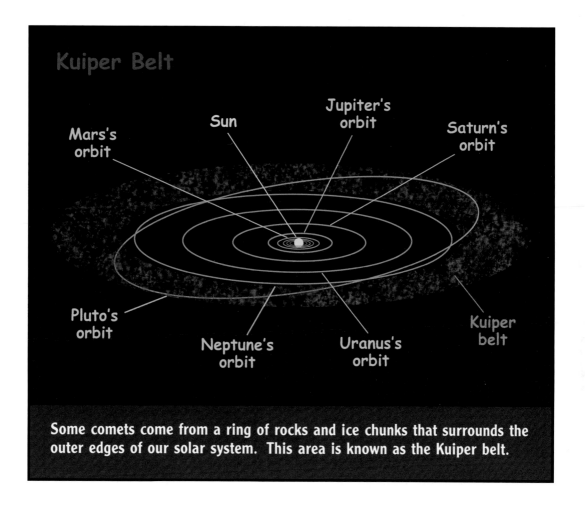

Kuiper Belt

Mars's orbit

Sun

Jupiter's orbit

Saturn's orbit

Pluto's orbit

Neptune's orbit

Uranus's orbit

Kuiper belt

Some comets come from a ring of rocks and ice chunks that surrounds the outer edges of our solar system. This area is known as the Kuiper belt.

Comets spend most of their time moving in darkness. Once in a while, gravity from a planet or nearby star changes a comet's orbit. Gravity is a force that pulls objects together. The comet's new path makes it move toward the nearby planet or star.

Nearing the Sun is dangerous for comets. Some fall into the Sun and are destroyed. Others pass near the Sun and part of them melts.

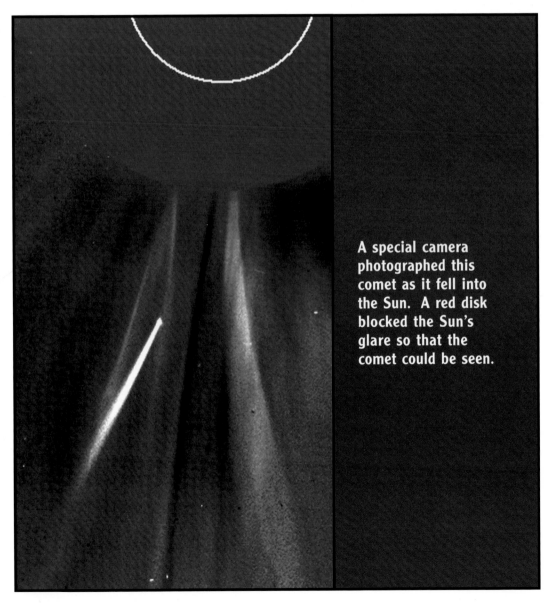

A special camera photographed this comet as it fell into the Sun. A red disk blocked the Sun's glare so that the comet could be seen.

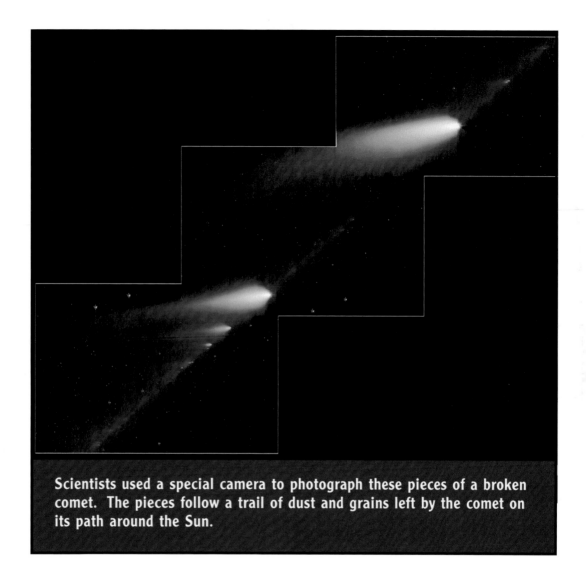

Scientists used a special camera to photograph these pieces of a broken comet. The pieces follow a trail of dust and grains left by the comet on its path around the Sun.

Comets almost totally melt away after many orbits. But dust and grains from the comet keep moving around the Sun. These may fall into Earth's atmosphere as meteors.

The Orion Nebula is a giant cloud of gas, dust, and rocks. The bright points are new stars that formed in the cloud. Scientists think that our solar system may have looked like this long ago.

Scientists believe that comets are very old. They think comets are pieces left from when the solar system began. This probably happened billions of years ago. It was a giant cloud of gas, dust, ice, and rocks.

Gravity caused the gas and other matter to come together. It made the cloud shrink. Most of the cloud of rocks, ice, and gases fell to the center and became the Sun. Smaller clumps formed the planets and moons. What was left over became comets and asteroids.

The solar system is full of chunks of rock and ice. This painting shows asteroids floating around the planet Uranus.

Most comets look like blurry stars. You may need a telescope (TEH-luh-skohp) to see them. A telescope makes objects that are far away look closer. One of the most famous comets is Halley's comet. This comet travels close to the Sun every 76 years. It will come back in 2061.

Halley's comet makes its 1986 visit to Earth.

Earth's moon (RIGHT) has been hit by millions of comets and meteors. They left round holes on the surface. What are these called?

CHAPTER 4
CRASHING INTO MOONS AND PLANETS

Sometimes a moon or planet gets in the way of a traveling comet or meteor. There is a great crash when this happens. The crash leaves a hole in the surface of the moon or planet. The hole is shaped like a bowl. This bowl-shaped hole is

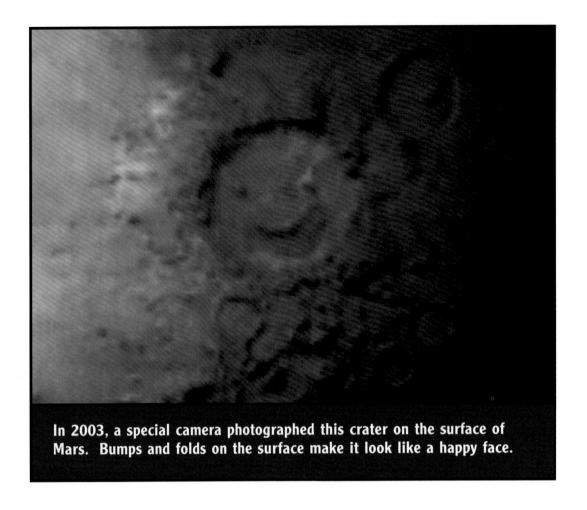

In 2003, a special camera photographed this crater on the surface of Mars. Bumps and folds on the surface make it look like a happy face.

Most of the other moons in the solar system have craters. So do the planets Mercury, Venus, and Mars. Jupiter, Saturn, Uranus, and Neptune do not have craters. They are made of gas. When an object hits them, the gas fills in what would have been a crater.

Earth has craters too. Most of them have been worn away by water and wind. But about 120 craters can still be found. One of Earth's craters is in Arizona. It is called Meteor Crater.

A meteorite made Meteor Crater in the Arizona desert. Scientists think the meteorite hit the desert at 28,600 miles (46,000 km) per hour.

Meteor Crater was made about 50,000 years ago. Scientists think that the meteorite that made the crater was made of metal. It weighed about 330,000 tons (300,000 metric tons). The crash blasted out a large crater 4,180 feet (1,275 meters) across. This is the length of about 90 school buses end to end.

This is a small piece of the meteorite that created Meteor Crater. It is made of mostly nickel and iron.

This huge
meteorite fell into
a pond in Canada
in 2008.

Earth is often hit by objects from space.
Most fall as very tiny pieces of dust or small
grains. These pieces are so small they can
hardly be seen. Sometimes comets and asteroids
strike Earth. These events were common in the
past. But now they are rare.

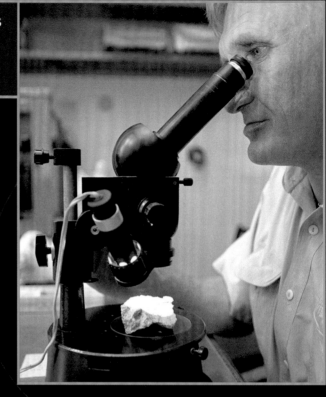
A Russian scientist examines a small piece of meteorite. What can we learn by studying meteorites?

CHAPTER 5

METEORITE AND COMET HUNTING

Meteorites and comets are some of the oldest objects in the solar system. They have changed little from when they were formed billions of years ago. Scientists study meteorites and comets to help learn how the universe began.

Scientists watch the sky for meteorites. They wait for one to crash. Then they try to collect the pieces. But finding the crash site and the pieces can be hard. A big meteorite may scatter its pieces over a wide area. Meteorites also strike Earth's oceans. They make a splash, and then they are gone.

Scientists tracked a meteorite to this backyard in Great Britain. When the meteorite hit the ground, it made a hole almost 5 feet (1.5 m) deep.

Finding meteorites is easy in Antarctica. This continent is covered by ice. Meteorites are dark. They stand out against the ice and snow. Scientists can spot the fallen meteorites. They ride out on snowmobiles and pick them up.

A researcher examines tiny pieces of a meteorite found in Antarctica.

In 1986, a European spacecraft flew close to Halley's comet. The spacecraft took this picture of the comet's nucleus and glowing coma.

Studying comets is harder. A comet that strikes Earth usually doesn't survive the crash. Scientists send spacecraft to study comets when they come near the Sun. A spacecraft is a machine that travels from Earth to outer space. Spacecraft from different countries flew near Halley's comet the last time it came near the Sun. The spacecraft flew near the comet. They took pictures and measurements.

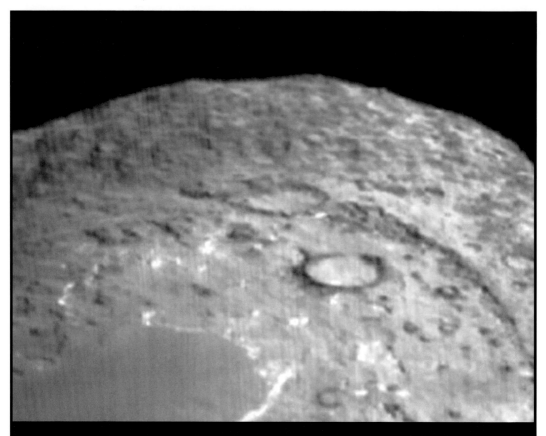

The *Deep Impact* spacecraft took this picture of the surface of comet Tempel 1 in 2005.

In 2005, the *Deep Impact* spacecraft from the United States went to the comet Tempel 1. The spacecraft had two parts. Part of the spacecraft took pictures. The other part crashed into the comet.

The crash kicked up material from the comet. The spacecraft took pictures of the material. The pictures showed that Tempel 1 is made of dust, ice, sand, and clay.

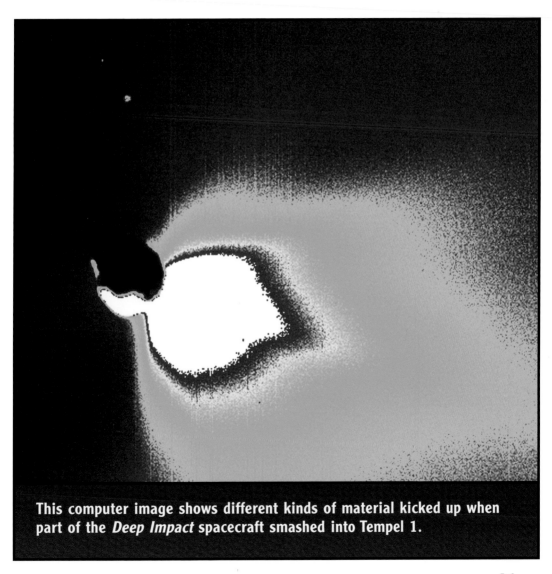

This computer image shows different kinds of material kicked up when part of the *Deep Impact* spacecraft smashed into Tempel 1.

A U.S. spacecraft named *Stardust* flew near comet Wild 2. *Stardust* gathered comet dust. Part of the spacecraft carried the dust back to Earth. Scientists studied the dust. It looked a lot like dust from meteorites.

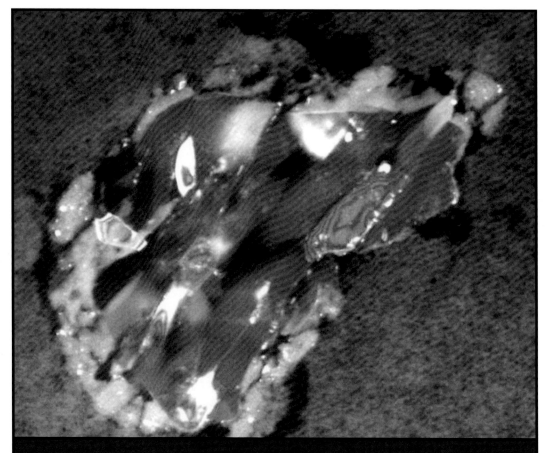

The spacecraft *Stardust* collected this piece of comet dust. Scientists discovered that it is made of a substance common on Earth and in meteorites.

This computer image shows the *Rosetta* spacecraft. It was launched in 2004. In 2014, it will cross a comet's orbit and launch a research vehicle that will land on the comet's surface.

More trips to comets are planned for the future. The materials in comets and meteorites have stories to tell. They tell the story of what our solar system was like when it formed.

ON SHARING A BOOK

When you share a book with a child, you show that reading is important. To get the most out of the experience, read in a comfortable, quiet place. Turn off the television and limit other distractions, such as telephone calls. Be prepared to start slowly. Take turns reading parts of this book. Stop occasionally and discuss what you're reading. Talk about the photographs. If the child begins to lose interest, stop reading. When you pick up the book again, revisit the parts you have already read.

BE A VOCABULARY DETECTIVE

The word list on page 5 contains words that are important in understanding the topic of this book. Be word detectives and search for the words as you read the book together. Talk about what the words mean and how they are used in the sentence. Do any of these words have more than one meaning? You will find the words defined in a glossary on page 46.

WHAT ABOUT QUESTIONS?

Use questions to make sure the child understands the information in this book. Here are some suggestions:

> What is a meteor called when it falls all the way to Earth? What are comets made of? How are craters formed? Why is studying comets harder than studying meteors?

If the child has questions, don't hesitate to respond with questions of your own, such as What do *you* think? Why? What is it that you don't know? If the child can't remember certain facts, turn to the index.

INTRODUCING THE INDEX

The index helps readers find information without searching through the whole book. Turn to the index on page 48. Choose an entry such as *asteroids* and ask the child to find out what asteroids are made of. Repeat with as many entries as you like. Ask the child to point out the differences between an index and a glossary. (The index helps readers find information, while the glossary tells readers what words mean.)

METEORS AND COMETS

BOOKS

Mist, Rosalind. *Could an Asteroid Hit the Earth?: Asteroids, Comets, Meteors, and More*. Chicago: Heinemann Library, 2006. Find out how asteroids and other space bodies could affect our planet.

Olien, Rebecca. *Exploring Meteors*. New York: PowerKids Press, 2007. Find out more about these amazing objects in the sky.

Orme, David. *Comets*. Winchester, UK: Ransom Publishing, 2007. Find out if comets and other space bodies are a danger to Earth.

Waxman, Laura Hamilton. *The Solar System*. Minneapolis: Lerner Publications Company, 2010. Learn more about the objects that share our solar system.

WEBSITES

NASA Photojournal
http://photojournal.jpl.nasa.gov/index.html
Click on the "Small Bodies" link to see pictures of comets and asteroids.

Solar System Exploration: Comets
http://solarsystem.nasa.gov/planets/profile.cfm?Object=Comets
Visit this site to learn even more about these icy space bodies.

Solar System Exploration: Meteoroids
http://solarsystem.nasa.gov/planets/profile.cfm?Object=Meteors
At this website you can get more information on meteoroids, meteors, and meteorites.

Windows to the Universe
http://www.windows.ucar.edu/windows.html
Find out more about comets, meteors, and the rest of the solar system. Click through "Our Solar System" to the "Comets" section, and then click on "Interactive Comet Animation" to build your own comet.

GLOSSARY

asteroids (A-stur-oydz): large chunks of space rock and metal that travel around the Sun. Asteroids can measure from 30 feet (9 m) to hundreds of miles across.

atmosphere (AT-muhs-feer): the layer of gases surrounding a planet or moon

coma (KOH-muh): the cloud of gas and tiny bits that forms around the icy center of a comet when it nears the Sun

comets (KAH-mits): large chunks of ice, dust, and rock that travel around the Sun

comet tail: a long stream of gas and dust that trails behind the comet's center

crater: a bowl-shaped dent in the surface of a planet or moon. A crater is blasted out when a meteorite or comet hits the surface.

gravity: a force that causes objects to be pulled toward one another

meteorites (MEE-tee-uh-ryets): meteors that land on Earth

meteoroids (MEE-tee-uh-royds): meteors before they come into Earth's atmosphere

meteors (MEE-tee-urz): tiny pieces of space rock or dust that burn up and glow brightly when they fall into Earth's atmosphere

meteor shower: dozens or hundreds of meteors that appear at one time in a part of the sky. Meteor showers happen at regular times during the year. They take place when Earth crosses a comet's path.

nucleus (NOO-klee-us): the icy, solid center of a comet

orbit: the path of a meteor, comet, or planet as it travels around the Sun. *Orbit* also means the path of a moon around its planet.

solar system: the Sun and the group of planets and other objects that travel around it

spacecraft: machines with or without people that travel from Earth into outer space

telescope (TEH-luh-skohp): an instrument that makes faraway objects appear bigger and closer

INDEX

Pages listed in **bold** type refer to photographs.